The Australian Womens Weekly Home Library

EDITOR: Maryanne Blacker

FOOD EDITOR: Pamela Clark

• • •

ASSOCIATE FOOD EDITOR:
Enid Morrison

HOME ECONOMIST: Jon Allen

EDITORIAL COORDINATOR: Elizabeth Hooper

KITCHEN ASSISTANT: Amy Wong

• • •

STYLIST: Jacqui Hing

PHOTOGRAPHER: Robert Clark

• • •

DESIGNER: Lisa Rowell

• • •

HOME LIBRARY STAFF:

ASSISTANT EDITOR: Beverley Hudec

ART DIRECTOR: Paula Wooller

EDITORIAL COORDINATOR: Fiona Nicholas

• • •

ACP PUBLISHER: Richard Walsh

ACP DEPUTY PUBLISHER: Nick Chan

• • •

Produced by The Australian Women's Weekly Home Library.
Typeset by ACP Colour Graphics Pty Ltd,. Printed by Dai
Nippon Co., Ltd in Japan.
Published by ACP Publishing, 54 Park Street Sydney.
♦ AUSTRALIA: Distributed by Network Distribution Company,
54 Park Street Sydney, (02) 282 8777.
♦ NEW ZEALAND: Distributed in New Zealand by Netlink
Distribution Company, 17B Hargreaves St, Level 5,
College Hill, Auckland 1, (9) 302 7616.
♦ UNITED KINGDOM: Distributed in the U.K.
by Australian Consolidated Press (UK) Ltd, 20 Galowhill Rd,
Brackmills, Northampton NN4 OEE, (0604) 760 456.
♦ CANADA: Distributed in Canada by Whitecap Books Ltd,
1086 West 3rd St,
North Vancouver V7P 3J6, (604) 9809852.
♦ SOUTH AFRICA: Distributed in South Africa by Intermag,
PO Box 57394, Springfield 2137, (011) 4933200.

• • •

Cake Decorating

Includes index.
ISBN 0 949128 47 3

1. Cake Decorating I. Title: Australian
Women's Weekly. (Series: Australian
Women's Weekly Home Library).

641.8'653

• • •

© A C P Publishing Pty Ltd
A.C.N. 053 273 546

• • •

FRONT COVER: Wedding Cake, page 72.
OPPOSITE: Wedding Cake, page 76.
BACK COVER: Father's Day Cake, page 112.

CAKE DECORATING
Made Easy

You need no special skills to decorate cakes superbly. In this
book, Mary Medway shows you how to achieve terrific effects
using everyday things such as greeting cards, spoon handles for
making patterns, flowers, ribbons and much more.
Instructions include step-by-step pictures for decorating
procedures to give a cake a professional finish with the
minimum of fuss. At the back of the book are recipes for a rich
fruit cake and icings, plus tips to give your work extra polish.
Cakes are numbered from 1 to 61 and include christenings,
birthdays, weddings, Christmas and special celebrations.

Pamela Clark

FOOD EDITOR

Mary Medway, who wrote this book for us, is a classical
cake decorator with more than 20 years' experience.
Known across the world for her skill and originality, she
has also written, *Cake Decorating – An Edible Art*. She is
pictured here with some of her prize-winning show entries.

BRITISH & NORTH AMERICAN READERS: Please note that Australian
cup and spoon measurements are metric. A quick conversion chart
appears on page 128.
A glossary explaining unfamiliar terms and ingredients appears on page 123.

CHRISTENINGS

No.1

1½ quantities fruit cake recipe
1½ quantities almond icing
1½ quantities soft icing
29cm x 37cm corner-cut rectangular covered board
greeting card
sugar syrup
artificial flowers
ribbon
lace

- Bake cake in deep 19cm x 27cm corner-cut rectangular cake pan.
- Cover cake with almond icing.
- Cover cake with soft icing.
- Position cake on board.
- Decorate as shown.

Cut card to appropriate shape. Brush back lightly with sugar syrup, position on cake. Decorate with flowers.

Make a looped bow, sew together, then stitch into position on band of ribbon.

Secure ribbon around cake with pins, join ends with sugar syrup. Remove pins when dry.

Gather lace, secure around cake with pins, sew joins together; remove the pins.

Picture shows sewing the ends of the lace together.

Mobile & cube from Adrienne & The Misses Bonney; card by courtesy of Hallmark Cards Aust Ltd.

No.2

1 quantity fruit cake recipe
1 quantity almond icing
1 quantity soft icing
pink colouring
29cm square covered board
patterned button
ribbon
lace
artificial flowers
- Bake cake in deep 19cm square cake pan.
- Cover cake with almond icing.
- Set aside a ball of soft icing (about 3cm in diameter) for bib.
- Colour remaining soft icing pink.
- Cover cake with pink soft icing.
- Position cake on board.
- Decorate as shown.

Roll white piece of reserved soft icing on a sheet of baking paper to a circle about 12cm in diameter. Use a cutter or lid to cut out a 10cm circle. Cut out a smaller circle to make bib shape. Leave bib on paper on flat surface to dry before painting.
To paint bib: Trace an appropriate picture onto greaseproof paper, use for copying onto set soft icing. Use diluted food colouring for painting. Leave to dry.

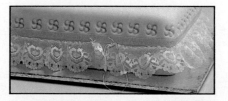

Use button to mark pattern into soft icing before it becomes firm. Secure ribbon around sides of cake with pins, sew ends together; remove pins. Gather lace slightly, secure around sides of cake with pins, sew edges together; remove pins.

Place bib in position on cake, place ribbon in position at points of bib. Arrange flowers at points of bib, gently push a length of gathered lace under edge of bib.

Pram & porcelain doll from Adrienne & The Misses Bonney

CHRISTENINGS

No.3

1 quantity fruit cake recipe
1 quantity almond icing
1 quantity soft icing
blue colouring
33cm hexagonal covered board
patterned button
ribbon
sugar syrup
greeting card

- Bake cake in deep 23cm hexagonal cake pan.
- Cover cake with almond icing.
- Colour soft icing pale blue.
- Cover cake with soft icing.
- Position cake on board.
- Decorate as shown.

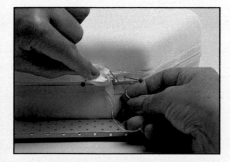

Secure ribbon around sides of cake with pins, sew ends together, sew bow into position; remove pins.

Gently press button into soft icing before it becomes firm.

Position picture on cake as shown, using a little sugar syrup.

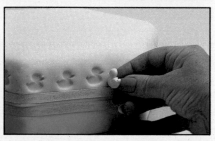

Roll scraps of soft icing into a sausage shape (about as thick as a pencil), long enough to encircle the cake. Press gently around base of cake, using a little sugar syrup to hold in place. Use a pasta wheel to make decoration.

Table from Techstyle; pillow from Adrienne & The Misses Bonney; rattle from Kate Finn Co; Silver mug from Whitehill Silver; card by courtesy of Valentine Sands Greetings

CHRISTENINGS

No.4

1 quantity fruit cake recipe
1 quantity almond icing
1 quantity soft icing
yellow colouring
29cm x 36cm oval covered board
greeting card
sugar syrup
artificial flowers
ribbon
lace

- Bake cake in deep 19cm x 26cm oval cake pan.
- Cover cake with almond icing.
- Colour soft icing lemon.
- Cover cake with soft icing.
- Position cake on board.
- Decorate as shown.

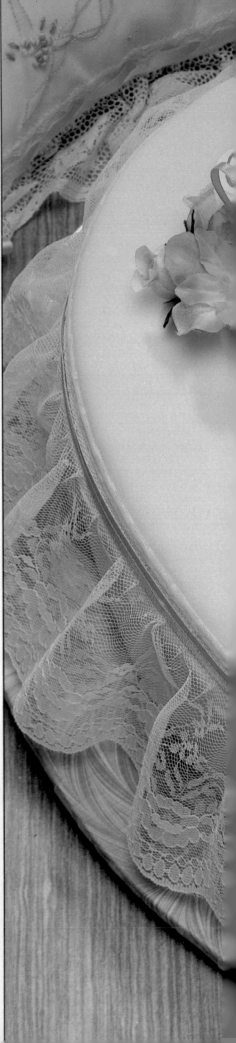

Secure cut-out from greeting card on top of cake with sugar syrup; decorate with flowers and ribbon.
   Secure lace around cake with pins, sew ends together; remove pins.

Sew bows in position on ribbon, secure around lace with pins, sew ends together; remove pins.

Pillow from Adrienne & The Misses Bonney; card by courtesy of Phil Taylor Greeting Cards

№.7

1 quantity fruit cake recipe
1 quantity almond icing
1 quantity soft icing
yellow colouring
27cm x 32cm rectangular covered board
ribbon
greeting card
sugar syrup

- Bake cake in deep 17cm x 22cm rectangular cake pan.
- Cover cake with almond icing.
- Colour soft icing pale yellow.
- Cover cake with soft icing.
- Position cake on board.
- Decorate as shown.

Secure ribbons around cake with pins. Sew firmly in position; remove pins when icing is firm.

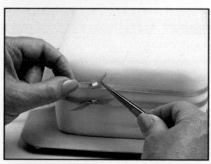

Tie knots over joins in ribbon.

Secure cut-out from card to cake with sugar syrup.

Ark & animals from Adrienne & The Misses Bonney; card by courtesy of Valentine Sands Greetings

No.8

1 quantity fruit cake recipe
1 quantity almond icing
1 quantity soft icing
29cm x 36cm oval covered board
lace
braid
greeting card
sugar syrup
artificial flowers

- Bake cake in deep 19cm x 26cm oval cake pan.
- Cover cake with almond icing.
- Cover cake with soft icing.
- Secure cake on board.
- Decorate as shown.

Secure a band of lace around side of cake with pins, join ends with sugar syrup; remove pins when dry.

Cover top edge of lace with braid, secure with pins, sew ends together; remove pins.

Secure cut-out card to top of cake with sugar syrup. Decorate with flowers.

Card by courtesy of Hallmark Cards Aust Ltd

No.9

1 quantity fruit cake recipe
1 quantity almond icing
1 quantity soft icing
pink colouring
33cm heart-shaped covered board
patterned button
ribbon
sugar syrup
red and green colourings
greeting card

- Bake cake in deep 23cm heart-shaped cake pan.
- Cover cake with almond icing.
- Colour soft icing pink.
- Cover cake with soft icing.
- Position cake on board.
- Decorate as shown.

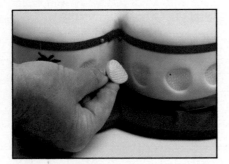

Use button to mark soft icing with pattern before it is firm.

Secure ribbon around cake with pins, join ends with sugar syrup; remove pins when dry.

Paint calyx of each strawberry with green colouring, paint fruit red.
    Secure cut-out from card on cake with sugar syrup.

Card by courtesy of Valentine Sands Greetings

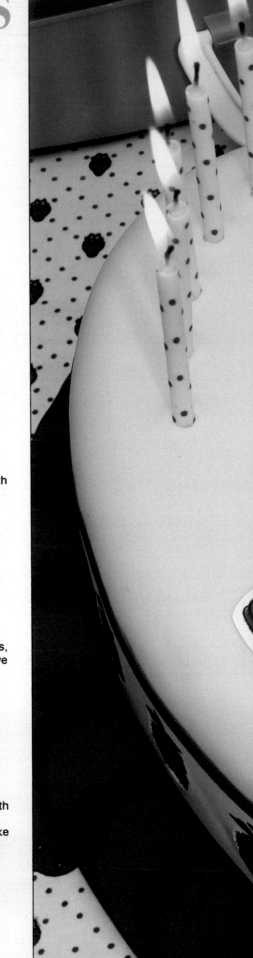

№ 10

1 quantity fruit cake recipe
1 quantity almond icing
1 quantity soft icing
29cm square covered board
blue, green, brown, yellow and pink colourings
ribbon
sugar syrup
fibralo pen
plastic eyes
greeting card

- Bake cake in deep 19cm square cake pan.
- Cover cake with almond icing.
- Reserve a ball (about the size of a tennis ball) of soft icing for the octopus and balloons. Colour remaining icing blue.
- Cover cake with blue soft icing.
- Position cake on board.
- Decorate as shown.

Measure ribbon for around cake, make a bow, stitch to ribbon, secure around base of cake.

Colour half the reserved icing different colours, roll into small balls, about the size of hazelnuts, press flat. Secure around sides and on top of cake with a little sugar syrup. This is best done before the balloons set. Use pen to draw the strings for balloons.

Colour remaining reserved soft icing green. Roll into sausage shape as shown, cut 8 tentacles. Gently push eyes into position, gently cut in a happy smile.

Picture shows how to arrange cut-outs from the card. This is best done on the cake before the octopus is set.

Background: Teddy & Friends

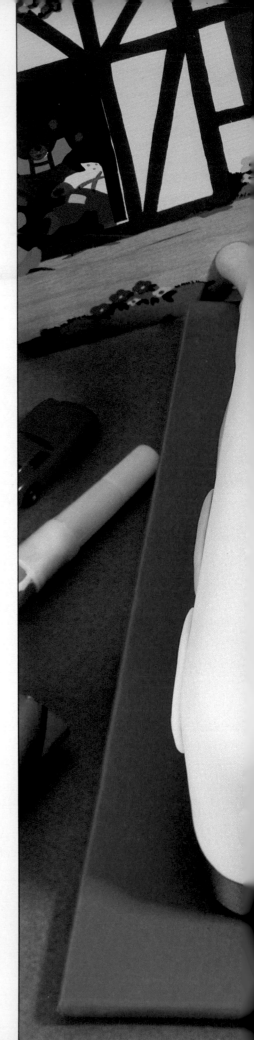

under 21

No. 11

1½ quantities fruit cake recipe
1½ quantities almond icing
1½ quantities soft icing
32cm x 37cm rectangular covered board
sugar syrup
patterned button
ribbon
greeting card

- Bake cake in deep 22cm x 27cm rectangular pan.
- Cover cake with almond icing.
- Cover cake with soft icing.
- Position cake on board.
- Decorate as shown.

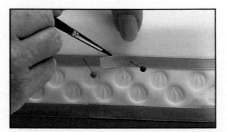

Press button into soft icing before it becomes firm.
  Secure ribbon around cake with pins; join ends with sugar syrup, allow to dry before removing pins.

Picture shows button used for pattern around sides of cake.

Secure cut-out from card on cake with sugar syrup.

Card by courtesy of Hallmark Cards Aust Ltd

No.12

1 quantity fruit cake recipe
1 quantity almond icing
1 quantity soft icing
32cm octagonal covered board
green, yellow, red and brown colourings
sugar syrup
patterned buttons
greeting card
ribbon

- Bake cake in deep 22cm octagonal cake pan.
- Cover cake with almond icing.
- Colour soft icing green.
- Cover cake with soft icing.
- Position cake on board.
- Decorate as shown.

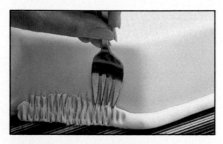

Roll scraps of soft icing into sausage shape about 1cm in diameter. Brush around base of cake with a little sugar syrup; place sausage in position around cake. Use a fork to make pattern in icing as shown.

Use buttons to make flowers and butterflies. This must be done before icing is set.

Use colourings to paint grass, flowers and butterflies. This is done when the icing has set. Secure cut-out from card on cake with sugar syrup. Secure ribbon loops with sugar syrup.

Background print & china bears from Teddy & Friends; table from Country Style Interiors; card by courtesy of Hallmark Cards Aust Ltd

No. 13

1½ quantities fruit cake recipe
1½ quantities almond icing
1½ quantities soft icing
yellow, brown, black and green colourings
33cm square covered board
polystyrene foam
rice paper
ribbon
sugar syrup
flowers

- Bake cake in deep 23cm square cake pan.
- Cover cake with almond icing.
- Colour soft icing pale yellow.
- Cover cake with soft icing.
- Position cake on board.
- Decorate as shown.

Cut a horseshoe shape from a small block of polystyrene foam, press into the unset soft icing. Leave to dry.

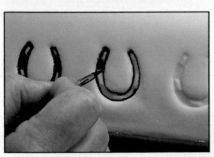

Paint horseshoe pattern on cake with brown colouring.

Trace outline onto rice paper, paint in details with colourings, allow to dry.

Trace rice paper shape onto cake, brush this area lightly with water, secure cut-out in position with pins; remove pins when dry. Secure ribbon around base of cake with pins, join ends with sugar syrup; remove pins when dry.

Decorate with flowers.

BIRTHDAYS
under 21

No.14

1½ quantities fruit cake recipe
1½ quantities almond icing
1½ quantities soft icing
34cm x 44cm book shaped covered board
greeting card
black and blue colourings
- Bake cake in 24cm × 34cm book cake pan.
- Cover cake with almond icing.
- Cover cake with soft icing.
- Position cake on board.
- Decorate as shown.

Use a knife to mark pages in the book, allow to dry.

Paint in sky.

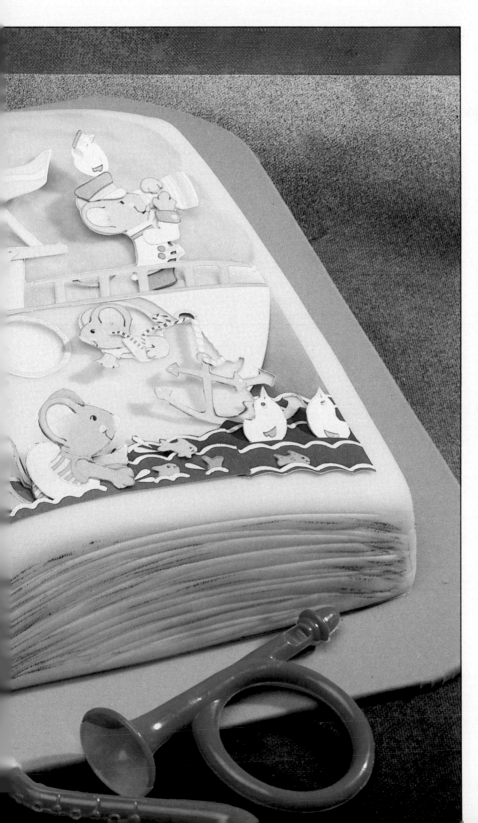

Cut out characters from the card, use small pieces of soft icing to hold them in an upright position for a 3 dimensional effect.

Use black colouring to mark pages in book.

BIRTHDAYS

under 21s

No.15

1½ quantities fruit cake recipe
1½ quantities almond icing
1½ quantities soft icing
33cm square covered board
lace
ribbon
sugar syrup
artificial flowers
patterned button
green colouring
fibralo pen

- Bake cake in deep 23cm square cake pan.
- Cover cake with almond icing.
- Cover cake with soft icing.
- Position cake on board
- Decorate as shown.

Secure lace and ribbon over corners of cake, secure at centre of each side with pins, join ends with sugar syrup, allow to dry; remove pins. Cover joins with a flower.

Press a pattern into the unset soft icing, using a button and a shaped wooden skewer, allow icing to dry.

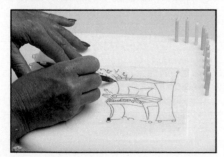

Trace pattern onto greaseproof paper, scratch onto set surface of cake. Draw outline with fibralo pen. Decorate with flowers.

1½ quantities fruit cake recipe
1½ quantities almond icing
1½ quantities soft icing
34cm x 42cm oval covered board
lace with inserted ribbon
rice paper
fibralo pen
artificial flowers
sugar syrup

- Bake cake in deep 24cm x 32cm oval cake pan.
- Cover cake with almond icing.
- Cover cake with soft icing.
- Position cake on board.
- Decorate as shown.

Secure lace around cake with pins, sew ends together, remove pins.

Trace picture onto rice paper with fibralo pen, cut out shape as shown. Paint in outline.

Secure flowers on cake with sugar syrup. Brush surface of cake with sugar syrup, place picture in position.

Ballet shoes: Bloch's Dance Wear

No.17

1 quantity fruit cake recipe
1 quantity almond icing
1 quantity soft icing
31cm heart-shaped covered board
lace
sugar syrup
ribbon
artificial flowers

- Bake cake in deep 21cm heart-shaped cake pan.
- Cover cake with almond icing.
- Cover cake with soft icing.
- Position cake on board.
- Decorate cake as shown.

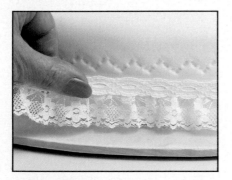

Use fancy teaspoon to mark pattern in unset icing. Secure lace around cake with pins, sew ends together; remove the pins.

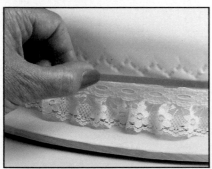

Secure ribbon around cake with pins, join ends with sugar syrup; remove pins when dry. Decorate cake with a heart of flowers.

Picture shows spoon used for making pattern around cake.

Champagne holder from Studio-Haus; glasses from Georg Jensen

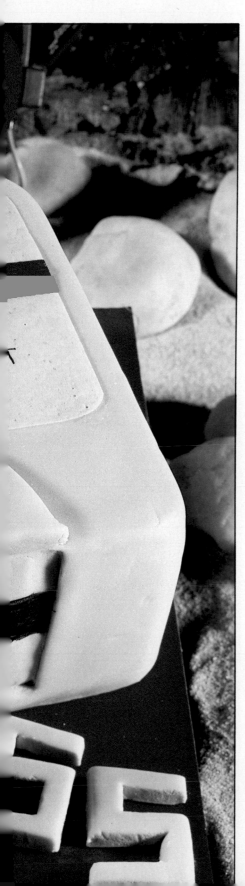

1 quantity fruit cake recipe
1 quantity almond icing
1 quantity soft icing
black colouring
27cm x 32cm rectangular
   covered board
rice paper
fibralo pens
sugar syrup
polystyrene foam

- Bake cake in deep 17cm x 22cm rectangular cake pan.
- Cover cake with almond icing.
- Colour soft icing grey
- Cover cake with soft icing.
- Position cake on board.
- Decorate as shown.

Cut rice paper to size and shape of cassette; use pens to mark patterns on paper.

Place rice paper in position, secure to cake with a little sugar syrup in each corner, hold in place with pins until dry, then remove pins.

Cut pattern into a cylinder of polystyrene foam as shown, use to mark pattern before icing is set.

When icing is dry, paint in tape with colouring.

Use a block of polystyrene foam to mark in area in front of tape; do this before the icing is set. Paint in tape when the icing is dry.

Use scraps of icing to make piece for top of cassette as shown, press into place using a little sugar syrup underneath.

No.19

1½ quantities fruit cake recipe
1½ quantities almond icing
1½ quantities soft icing
32cm x 37cm rectangular covered board
green, blue, red, yellow, brown and black colourings
sugar syrup

- Bake cake in deep 22cm x 27cm rectangular cake pan.
- Cover cake with almond icing.
- Colour half the soft icing green.
- Colour half the remaining soft icing blue.
- Use remaining soft icing for various additions to bag.
- Cover top two-thirds of cake with green soft icing, use picture as a guide for making flap and pouch.
- Cover lower third of cake with blue soft icing for bed roll.
- Use remaining soft icing to make straps, water carrier, spade etc. Use sugar syrup to help position additions to pack.

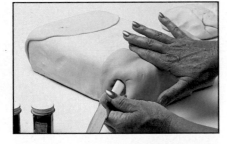

Press and push bed roll into shape.

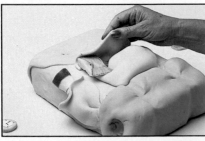

Form pouch, fold flap over.

Position straps (and other additions); secure with sugar syrup, if necessary.

No. 20

1½ quantities fruit cake recipe
1½ quantities almond icing
1½ quantities soft icing
33cm square covered board
gathered lace with inserted ribbon
embroidered daisy motif
red, yellow and green colourings
artificial flowers
ribbon

- Bake cake in deep 23cm square cake pan.
- Cover cake with almond icing.
- Colour soft icing lemon.
- Cover cake with soft icing.
- Position cake on board.
- Decorate as shown.

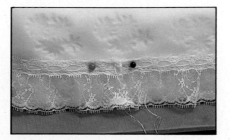

Secure lace around cake with pins, sew ends together; remove pins.

Picture shows how to press motif gently into side of unset soft icing. Leave icing to set.

Paint daisy motif with colourings. Arrange flowers and ribbon as shown.

Glass from Kosta Boda; frame from Graphis Art & Framing; table and pedestal from Techstyle

BIRTHDAYS
21st

Best Wishes

Chris

congratulations Christopher happy birthday

ongratulations Twenty one hip hip hoor

No.21

1½ quantities fruit cake recipe
1½ quantities almond icing
1½ quantities soft icing
30cm x 55cm rectangular covered board
fibralo pens
ribbon
sugar syrup

- Bake cake in deep 40cm long key-shaped cake pan.
- Cover cake with almond icing.
- Cover cake with soft icing.
- Position cake on board.
- Decorate as shown.

Glasses from Studio-Haus; background table from Kerry Trollope Antiques; picture from Graphis Art & Framing

We used a technique called flooding to give the 3 dimensional look to the cake's decorations. This is done by using a wet mixture of various colours of royal icing and brushing or piping the icing onto a pattern or picture. Soft icing, broken down with cold boiled water, can also be used. When it is completely dry, more details are painted on. This technique takes skill and practice but is fun to try. Start with a sample picture cut from a card or magazine. The 3 dimensional look can also be achieved by cutting out various pieces of an appropriate card and supporting them with small pieces of soft icing. Position cut-outs at different angles for a pleasing effect.

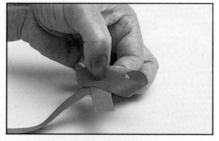

To make bow, loop ribbon as shown.

Sew loops securely into position, sew to end of ribbon.

Secure ribbon around cake with pins, join ends with sugar syrup, remove pins when dry. When icing is set, print or write messages around cake with fibralo pens.

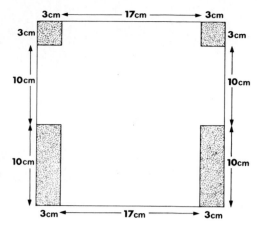

Cut out 3cm square corner pieces; these are not required for this cake. Cut out the 3cm x 10cm pieces, place against uncut 10cm portions of cake, join with jam. Trim to rounded shape for headlights.

1½ quantities fruit cake recipe
apricot jam
1½ quantities almond icing
1½ quantities soft icing
black and blue colourings
33cm square covered board
aluminium foil
silver ribbon
sugar syrup
black ribbon

- Bake cake in deep 23cm square cake pan.
- Cut cake as shown in diagram
- Join piece of cake with sieved apricot jam.
- Cut headlights into rounded shape.
- Cover cake with almond icing.
- Remove a ball of soft icing about 5cm in diameter.
- Colour remaining soft icing grey with black colouring.
- Cover cake with grey soft icing.
- Position cake on board.
- Decorate cake as shown.

Roll scraps of soft icing into sausage shapes, place around headlights. Cut circles from foil, use for headlights.

Paint sides of grille blue, leave headlights grey, paint top black.

Place strips of silver ribbon on top of cake while colouring is damp. Use a piece of ribbon to cover ends of strips. It may be necessary to hold the ribbon securely with pins. Be sure to remove pins and ribbon before cake is cut.

Roll scraps of soft icing to a rectangular shape for number plate, leave to dry, paint black. Roll out reserved white soft icing, cut out numbers and letters for number plate. Secure numbers and letters to number plate with a little sugar syrup after colouring is dry.

Make a mascot for the grille with scraps of soft icing, leave to dry before securing with sugar syrup.

Secure black ribbon around base of cake with pins, join ends with sugar syrup, remove pins when dry.

Model cars, spectacles, cap & car key holder from John Newell Porsche Centre.

No.23

1½ quantities fruit cake recipe
1½ quantities almond icing
1½ quantities soft icing
black colouring
33cm square covered board

- Bake cake in deep 23cm square cake pan.
- Cover cake with almond icing.
- Reserve a ball of soft icing about 5cm in diameter.
- Colour remaining soft icing grey.
- Cover cake with grey soft icing.
- Position cake on board.
- Decorate cake as shown.

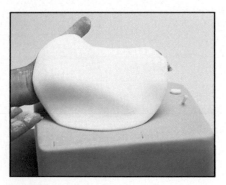

Make various switches as shown from reserved white soft icing. Mark in areas for panels, etc.

Roll remaining white soft icing into a circle on surface dusted with sifted icing sugar. Cut circle to correct size using a cake pan or plate as a guide. Lift circle carefully onto cake.

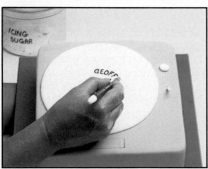

When record is dry, write in centre.

Paint record and panels as shown. Make arm for player from scraps of soft icing, leave to dry before painting. Place arm in position on cake.

No. 24

1 quantity fruit cake recipe
1 quantity almond icing
1 quantity soft icing
27cm x 32cm rectangular covered board
fibralo pen
ribbons
greeting card
sugar syrup

- Bake cake in deep 17cm × 22cm rectangular cake pan.
- Cover cake with almond icing.
- Cover cake with soft icing.
- Position cake on board.
- Decorate cake as shown.

Picture shows piping tube used to mark circles for wheels. Mark circles around side of cake before icing is set. Spokes of wheels were marked in with fibralo pen.

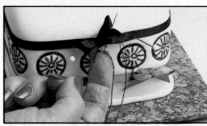

Sew bows into position on ends of ribbons. Secure ribbons around cake with pins, sew ends; remove pins.

Secure cut-out from card on cake with sugar syrup.

Knife from Georg Jensen Silver

No. 25

1 quantity fruit cake recipe
1 quantity almond icing
1 quantity soft icing
35cm triangular-shaped covered board
green, brown, red, blue, black, yellow and pink colourings
cornflour

- Bake cake in 25cm fan-shaped cake pan.
- Cut curved side from fan to make triangular-shaped cake.
- Cover cake with almond icing.
- Reserve a quarter of the soft icing for making billiard balls.
- Cover cake with remaining soft icing.
- Paint brown section of cake first, then green section.
- Position billiard balls before soft icing is set.
- Position cake on board.
- Make billiard balls as shown.

Remove mechanism from an ice cream scoop. Rub inside bowl of scoop with cornflour. Take a ball of soft icing about 2cm in diameter, press it evenly into bowl of scoop, forming a hollow. Trim away excess soft icing, as shown.

Fill cavity in soft icing with cornflour, level top with knife.

Turn ball onto flat surface. When dry, lift shape away from cornflour. Make remaining balls. Paint various colours, as shown.

Pewter mugs from Studio-Haus

No.26

1 quantity fruit cake recipe
1 quantity almond icing
1 quantity soft icing
33cm x 40cm oval covered board
ribbon
sugar syrup
greeting card
1 small bottle port
green, yellow, purple and brown
    colourings
- Bake cake in deep 23cm round cake pan.
- Cover cake with almond icing.
- Reserve about a fifth of the soft icing for decorations.
- Cover cake with remaining soft icing.
- Position cake on board as shown.
- Decorate cake as shown.

Sew bow onto end of ribbon, secure around cake with pins, join ends with sugar syrup. Remove pins when dry. Secure cut-out from card on cake with sugar syrup.

Roll out a small portion of reserved soft icing on surface dusted with sifted icing sugar, cut out leaves. Dry leaves on a soft tissue or cotton wool, dry in interesting shapes.

Mould another piece of reserved icing into a cone shape. Make grapes, press onto cone, as shown.

Paint grapes and leaves when dry. Arrange on cake with port, as shown.

No.27

1 quantity fruit cake recipe
1 quantity soft icing
1 quantity almond icing
27cm x 32cm rectangular covered board
red and black colourings
1 sheet gelatine
aluminium foil
rice paper
fibralo pen

- Bake cake in deep 17cm x 22cm rectangular cake pan.
- Cut cake into a slightly smaller rectangular shape.
- Make a roll of soft icing and position on 1 end of camera for hand-grip.
- Cover cake with almond icing.
- Cover cake with soft icing.
- Position cake on board.
- Decorate cake as shown.

Cut a circle from scraps of soft icing for the base of the lens. Place in position as shown. Use a meat mallet to mark hand-grip.

Paint inside of lens with black colouring, cut gelatine sheet to fit, place in position.

Mark in view finder, etc. Cut pieces of foil to fit marked areas. Cut another circle from soft icing to fit on top of base of lens, place in position, mark in groove to be painted red later.

Paint camera black, paint in red groove, place pieces of foil in position while colouring is wet. Write names on rice paper with fibralo pen, attach to damp cake with pins; remove pins when dry. Make piece of cord for camera from soft icing scraps, paint black when dry.

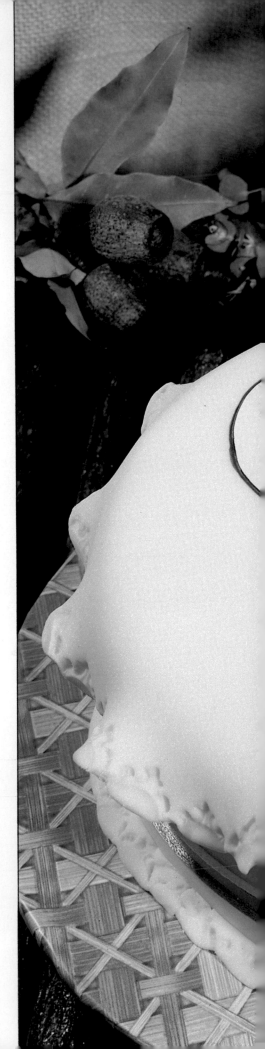

No. 28

1 quantity fruit cake recipe
1 quantity almond icing
1½ quantities soft icing
33cm round covered board
greeting card
sugar syrup
ribbon

- Bake cake in deep 23cm round cake pan.
- Cover cake with almond icing.
- Cover cake with two thirds of the soft icing.
- Position cake on board.
- Decorate as shown.

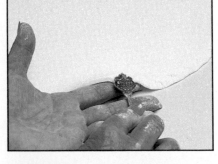

Roll out remaining soft icing to a circle with 28cm diameter. Use the handle of a teaspoon to make a decorative edge.

Lift the circle of icing carefully onto the cake, gently arrange icing into frills with fingers dusted lightly with sifted icing sugar.

Roll scraps of soft icing into sausage shape about the thickness of a pencil, place around base of cake. Press the spoon handle into the icing, as shown.
 Secure cut-out from card in position with sugar syrup; outline cut-out if desired with pen after icing is set.
 Secure ribbons around cake, cover joins with bows.

Background table from Mid-City House & Garden; card by courtesy of Valentine Sands Greetings

No.29

1 quantity fruit cake recipe
1 quantity almond icing
1 quantity soft icing
green and blue colourings
32cm round covered board
braid
ribbon
lace
sugar syrup
artificial flowers
guipure lace motif

- Bake cake in deep 22cm 5-petal cake pan.
- Cover cake with almond icing.
- Colour soft icing aqua with colourings.
- Cover cake with soft icing.
- Position cake on board.
- Decorate cake as shown.

Secure braid, ribbon and lace with pins at each scallop around cake. Brush a little sugar syrup behind each piece of ribbon, etc. at each scallop. When dry, remove pins.

Arrange flowers and ribbon loops on cake. Brush back of lace motif with sugar syrup, position on cake.

Cake server from Studio-Haus

No.30

1 quantity fruit cake recipe
1 quantity almond icing
1 quantity soft icing
brown colouring
29cm square covered board
patterned button
artificial flowers

- Bake cake in deep 19cm square cake pan.
- Cover cake with almond icing.
- Colour soft icing off-white.
- Cover cake with soft icing.
- Position cake on board.
- Decorate cake as shown.

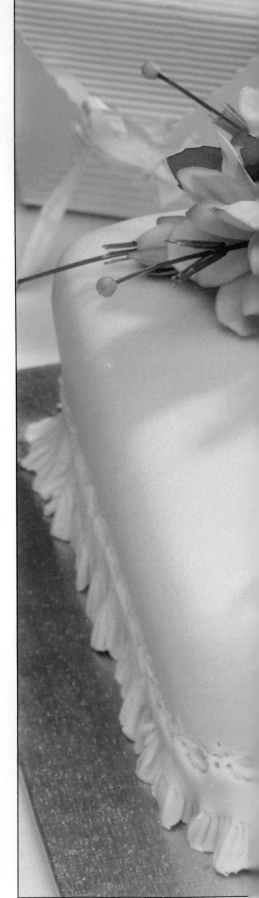

Make frill by rolling out scraps of soft icing into a circle. Use a fluted flan tin like a cutter to cut a circle from the soft icing circle.

Use a plate or lid to cut a smaller circle from the centre to make a band of fluted soft icing. Cut into pieces about 6cm long. Use a knitting needle to mark grooves in soft icing.

Straighten plain band of frill, use knitting needle to arrange frills evenly. Brush underside of plain band of frill with a little sugar syrup. Press gently into position on cake, smooth plain part onto side of cake. Repeat with more pieces of soft icing.

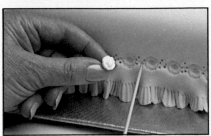

Use button to make pattern in unset soft icing along the join. Make pattern with knitting needle or skewer. Arrange flowers on cake.

Glasses from Studio-Haus

No.31

1 quantity fruit cake recipe
1 quantity almond icing
1 quantity soft icing
brown colouring
29cm x 37cm corner-cut rectangular covered board
lace
patterned button
artificial flowers
ribbon

- Bake cake in deep corner-cut 19cm x 27cm rectangular cake pan.
- Cover cake with almond icing.
- Colour soft icing off-white.
- Cover cake with soft icing.
- Position cake on board.
- Decorate cake as shown.

Secure lace around cake with pins, bringing the lace down towards the board in the front of the cake. Sew ends of lace together; remove pins.

Picture shows button used to mark pattern in unset soft icing.

Cover joins in lace with a flower. Arrange flowers and loops of ribbon on top of cake.

Knife from Georg Jensen Silver

No.32

1½ quantities fruit cake recipe
1½ quantities almond icing
1½ quantities soft icing
34cm x 43cm diamond-shaped covered board
sugar syrup
lace edging with inserted ribbon
artificial flowers
patterned button
greeting card
rice paper
blue and pink colourings
blue, pink and black fibralo pens
piping gel

- Bake cake in deep 24cm x 33cm diamond-shaped cake pan.
- Cover cake with almond icing.
- Cover cake with soft icing.
- Position cake on board.
- Decorate cake as shown.

Use scraps of soft icing to make a roll about the thickness of a pencil and long enough to encircle base of cake. Use handle of a teaspoon to make a pattern, as shown. Use a little sugar syrup to secure roll in position.

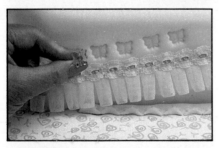

Before soft icing is set, place lace around cake; hold in position on opposite corners with "stems" of flowers and leaves. Use button to make pattern on sides of cake.

Trace picture onto rice paper with blue and pink pens. Write message on rice paper, cut out message and picture. Scratch outline of both onto cake's set surface. Use coloured piping gel to paint in details of pictures. Brush in areas where rice paper is to be positioned with a little water, place cut-outs in position, secure with pins until dry; remove pins. Paint butterflies around sides of cake with piping gel.

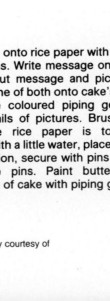

Background fabric from Wilson Fabrics; glasses from Studio-Haus; card by courtesy of Valentine Sands Greetings

WEDDINGS

engagement

No.33

1½ quantities fruit cake recipe
1½ quantities almond icing
1½ quantities soft icing
brown colouring
29cm x 37cm corner-cut rectangular covered board
glass
artificial flower
lace
sugar syrup
ribbon
rice paper
fibralo pen

- Bake cake in deep 19cm x 27cm corner-cut rectangular cake pan.
- Cover cake with almond icing.
- Colour soft icing off-white.
- Cover cake with soft icing.
- Position cake on board.
- Decorate cake as shown.

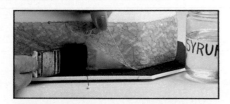

Position glass and flower on cake before soft icing is set. Secure lace around cake with pins, join ends with sugar syrup; remove pins when dry.

Sew a bow onto ribbon, secure ribbon around base of cake with pins, sew ends together. Remove pins.

Trace lettering onto rice paper with fibralo pen.

Cut out around lettering, scratch area onto set surface of cake. Brush in the area with a little water, position rice paper on damp surface. Secure with pins until dry; remove pins.

Background from Adrienne & The Misses Bonney

engagement

No.34

1 quantity fruit cake recipe
1 quantity almond icing
1 quantity soft icing
caramel colouring
29cm x 36cm oval covered board
gathered lace with inserted ribbon
patterned button
greeting card
sugar syrup
artificial flowers
ribbon

- Bake cake in deep 19cm x 26cm oval cake pan.
- Cover cake with almond icing.
- Colour soft icing caramel.
- Cover cake with soft icing.
- Position cake on board.
- Decorate cake as shown.

Secure lace around cake with pins, sew ends together; remove pins.

Mark pattern with button in soft icing before it sets.

Secure cut-out from card on top of cake with sugar syrup. Decorate with flowers and loops of ribbon as shown.

Cake server from Whitehill Silver; table from Techstyle; card by courtesy of Coolabah Gallery Pty Ltd, copyright The Andrew Brownsword Collection 1987

No.35

1½ quantities fruit cake recipe
1½ quantities almond icing
1½ quantities soft icing
blue colouring
33cm square covered board
patterned button
ribbon
sugar syrup
artificial flowers

- Bake cake in deep 23cm square cake pan.
- Cover cake with almond icing.
- Colour soft icing blue.
- Cover cake with soft icing.
- Position cake on board.
- Decorate cake as shown.

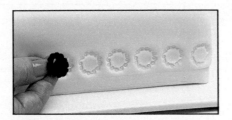

Use button to make pattern in unset soft icing around sides of cake.

Secure ribbon around base of cake with pins, join ends with sugar syrup; remove pins when dry.

Sew loops of ribbon together, gently push loops into unset soft icing; secure with a little sugar syrup. Secure flowers to cake with sugar syrup.

Champagne glasses from Studio-Haus; table from Wentworth Antiques

No.36

2 quantities fruit cake recipe
2 quantities almond icing
2 quantities soft icing
2 rectangular covered boards; the small board is 18cm x 23cm,
    the large board is 36cm x 41cm
white dressing gown cord
lace edging
2 patterned buttons, small and large
3 wooden skewers
artificial flowers
ribbon

- Bake cakes in 2 deep rectangular cake pans; the small pan is 12cm x 17cm, the large pan is 22cm x 27cm.
- Cover cakes with almond icing.
- Cover cakes with soft icing.
- Position cakes on boards.
- Decorate cakes as shown.

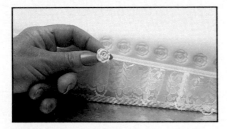

Secure cord around base of cakes with pins, sew ends together; remove pins. Secure lace edging around sides of cakes with pins, sew ends together; remove pins.

Use buttons to mark pattern on sides of cakes before the icing is set. Use the small button on the small cake and the large button on the large cake.

Trace the size of the small cake onto a piece of greaseproof paper, use this pattern to determine position of skewers so they will support the top tier. Cut points from skewers.

Push skewers (through to the board) into the large cake to measure depth, add another 7cm to this length. Remove skewers and cut off neatly.

Tie cord to skewers with cotton, wind around skewers, secure with adhesive tape.

Push skewers into large cake, as shown. Arrange flowers and loops of ribbon on cakes, place top tier in position.

Handkerchief and horse shoe from Adrienne & The Misses Bonney

WEDDINGS

No.37

2 quantities fruit cake recipe
2 quantities almond icing
2 quantities soft icing
21cm round covered board
38cm x 46cm oval covered board
2 patterned buttons, small and large
lace with inserted ribbon
artificial flowers
glass bowl
3 wooden skewers

- Bake cakes in 2 deep cake pans; the small round cake is 15cm in diameter, the large oval cake is 24cm x 32cm.
- Cover cakes with almond icing.
- Cover cakes with soft icing.
- Position cakes on boards.
- Decorate cakes as shown.

Use buttons to make pattern in unset soft icing around cakes. Use the small button on the small cake and the large button on the large cake. Secure lace around cakes with pins, sew ends together; remove pins.

Picture shows button used to make pattern on cakes.

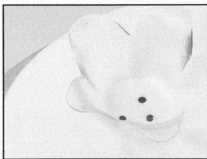

Arrange flowers on large cake. Determine position for bowl to support small cake. Cut points from skewers, push skewers into cake (through to the board) in the area to support the bowl. Mark skewers level with the surface of the cake, remove skewers and cut off neatly. Skewers must be all the same length. Place bowl in position on skewers.

Arrange flowers on top tier, place top tier in position.

No.38

Cover the 3 boards used for this cake with white Contact plastic, cover tops and bottoms. Crown of top hat is formed by joining 2 cakes.

2 quantities fruit cake recipe
3 quantities almond icing
3 quantities soft icing
40cm round covered board
black colouring
sugar syrup
17cm (approximately) round
  covered board
28cm round covered board
grosgrain ribbon
plastic stand 18cm high
white scarf
fresh flowers

● Bake 2 cakes in deep 18cm round cake pans; bake 1 cake in deep 20cm round cake pan.
● Trim the top of the large cake to represent the crown of the bonnet.
● Cover crown of bonnet with about a third of the almond icing.

Cover large board with about a quarter of the soft icing; trim and smooth the edges neatly.

Cover crown of bonnet with about a third of remaining soft icing. Place in centre of soft icing-covered board. Leave to dry.

Trim the tops of the 2 smaller cakes so they are flat. Cut a circle of almond icing large enough to cover the top of 1 of the cakes. Colour remaining soft icing grey.

Cut a circle of grey soft icing large enough to cover almond icing; secure to almond icing with sugar syrup.

Cover grey soft icing with the 17cm board. This board must fit the diameter of the cake exactly, so the cakes can be separated easily for cutting.

Secure remaining cake to board on top of the other cake. Cover the joined cakes entirely with the remaining almond icing.

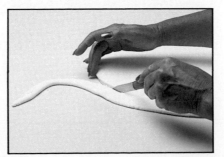

Cover the 28cm board with about a quarter of the grey soft icing.

Roll remaining grey soft icing to a rectangular shape, trim and cut to fit the side of the top hat. Brush side of cake with sugar syrup, roll over soft icing as shown. Rub joins gently with fingers to blend as evenly as possible.

Stand cake on grey soft icing-covered board.

Roll scraps of remaining grey soft icing to a circle, cut to fit top of top hat. Brush almond icing lightly with sugar syrup, place circle of grey soft icing in position, rub joins with fingers to blend as evenly as possible.

Make a flat bow from the grosgrain ribbon, sew onto the band, secure around the cake with pins, sew ends together. Place on plastic stand.

Tie scarf around bonnet, decorate with flowers as late as possible.

No.39

2 quantities fruit cake recipe
2 quantities almond icing
2 quantities soft icing
2 diamond-shaped covered boards; the small board is 21cm x 31cm,
   the large board is 38cm x 47cm
sugar syrup
guipure lace
4 wooden skewers
4 plastic pillars
fresh flowers

- Bake cakes in 2 deep diamond-shaped cake pans; the small pan is 15cm x 25cm, the large pan is 24cm x 33cm.
- Cover cakes with almond icing.
- Cover cakes with soft icing.
- Position cakes on boards.
- Decorate cakes as shown.

Make rolls from scraps of soft icing about the thickness of a pencil, secure around cakes with a little sugar syrup. Make pattern in rolls with the handle of a teaspoon.

Brush back of lace with sugar syrup, secure around cakes with pins, as shown. Remove pins when dry.

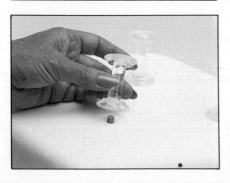

Trace the size of the small cake pan onto greaseproof paper; use this pattern to determine position of skewers so they will support the top tier. Cut points from skewers. Push skewers (through to the board) into the large cake to measure depth, add another 7mm to this length. Remove skewers and cut off neatly. Push skewers into cake, place pillars in position. Arrange flowers on cakes as late as possible.

Fabric from The Vintage Clothing Shop; glasses from Kosta Boda

No.40

Cover boards both sides for this cake.

3 quantities fruit cake recipe
3 quantities almond icing
3 quantities soft icing
3 hexagonal covered boards; small is 21cm,
    medium is 26cm; large is 39cm
47cm x 86cm rectangular covered board
2 plastic cake stands; small is 8cm high;
    large is 18cm high
ribbon
sugar syrup
lace flouncing
fresh flowers

- Bake cakes in 3 deep hexagonal cake pans, the small is 15cm, the medium is 20cm and the large is 25cm.
- Cover cakes with almond icing.
- Cover cakes with soft icing.
- Position cakes on boards.
- Decorate cakes as shown.

Secure ribbon around base of cakes with pins, join ends with sugar syrup. Remove pins when dry.

Wrap lace flouncing around cakes twice, secure with pins, sew edges together; remove pins.

Secure band of ribbon between bands of flouncing, secure with pins, sew ends together; remove pins.
    Position cakes on stands, as shown on rectangular board. Decorate with flowers as late as possible.

Champagne bucket from R. P. Symons; glasses from Kosta Boda; bride and groom and lace on table from The Vintage Clothing Shop

No.41

1½ quantities fruit cake recipe
1½ quantities almond icing
1½ quantities soft icing
34cm x 42cm oval covered board
lace
ribbon
fresh flowers

- Bake cake in deep 24cm x 32cm oval cake pan.
- Cover cake with almond icing.
- Cover cake with soft icing.
- Position cake on board.
- Decorate cake as shown.

Mark border around cake with teaspoon handle. Secure lace around cake with pins, sew ends together; remove pins.

Secure bands of ribbon around cake with pins, join ends with sugar syrup. Remove pins when dry.

Picture shows teaspoon handle used for pattern. Position flowers on cake as late as possible.

Lace from The Vintage Clothing Shop

WEDDINGS
anniversary

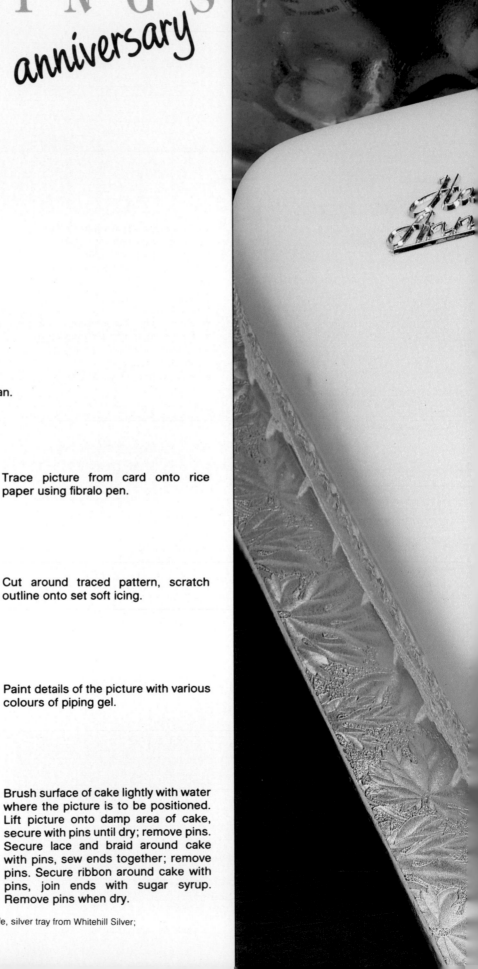

No.42

1 quantity fruit cake recipe
1 quantity almond icing
1 quantity soft icing
29cm square covered board
greeting card
rice paper
fibralo pen
pink and green colourings
piping gel
lace
braid
ribbon

- Bake cake in deep 19cm square cake pan.
- Cover cake with almond icing.
- Cover cake with soft icing.
- Position cake on board.
- Decorate cake as shown.

Trace picture from card onto rice paper using fibralo pen.

Cut around traced pattern, scratch outline onto set soft icing.

Paint details of the picture with various colours of piping gel.

Brush surface of cake lightly with water where the picture is to be positioned. Lift picture onto damp area of cake, secure with pins until dry; remove pins. Secure lace and braid around cake with pins, sew ends together; remove pins. Secure ribbon around cake with pins, join ends with sugar syrup. Remove pins when dry.

Table from Wentworth Antiques; champagne bucket, knife, silver tray from Whitehill Silver; champagne glasses from Studio-Haus

No. 43

1 quantity fruit cake recipe
1 quantity almond icing
1 quantity soft icing
33cm round covered board
ribbon
green, red, yellow and blue colourings
sugar syrup
red and green fibralo pens

- Bake cake in deep 23cm round cake pan.
- Cover cake with almond icing.
- Cover cake with soft icing.
- Position cake on board.
- Decorate cake as shown.

Use scraps of rolled-out soft icing to cut out holly leaves. Twist leaves into interesting shapes, paint when dry. Mould parcels, bells, bonbons, etc. from more scraps of soft icing; paint when dry.

Make bow by sewing loops together, position small holly berries in centre of bow.

Make frill by rolling out scraps of soft icing into a circle. Use a fluted flan tin like a cutter to cut a circle from the soft icing.

Use a plate or lid to cut a smaller circle from the centre to make a band of fluted soft icing. Cut into pieces about 6cm long. Use a knitting needle to mark grooves in soft icing.

Straighten plain band of frill; use knitting needle to arrange frills evenly. Brush underside of plain band of frill with a little sugar syrup. Press gently into position on cake, smooth plain part onto side of cake. Repeat with more pieces of soft icing.

Cover joins of frill with ribbon, secure with pins, join ends with sugar syrup. Remove pins when dry.

Paint in holly and berries with fibralo pens. Decorate top of cake as shown.

Sleigh from Adrienne & The Misses Bonney; tree and gift box from Swing Gifts

valentine's day

No.47

1 quantity fruit cake recipe
1 quantity almond icing
1 quantity soft icing
31cm heart-shaped covered board
braid
lace
greeting card
rice paper
fibralo pens
red and green colourings
piping gel

- Bake cake in deep 21cm heart-shaped cake pan.
- Cover cake with almond icing.
- Cover cake with soft icing.
- Position cake on board.
- Decorate cake as shown.

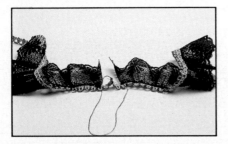

Cut the braid 4cm longer than the distance around the cake. Gather lace, sew it onto the braid.

Secure lace and braid around cake with pins. Push ends of braid into unset soft icing in centre indent of heart shape. Remove pins.

Trace flowers from card or picture onto rice paper using fibralo pens, cut out around shape of flowers. Place outline on set surface of cake, scratch outline onto icing. Paint rose using coloured piping gel. Brush inside the outlined area on cake lightly with water, place picture in position.

Table from Kerry Trollope Antiques; champagne bucket and knife from Whitehill Silver

No.48

1 quantity fruit cake recipe
1 quantity almond icing
1 quantity soft icing
pink colouring
33cm round covered board
guipure lace
doily
ribbon
sugar syrup
lace
artificial flowers

- Bake cake in deep 23cm round cake pan.
- Cover cake with almond icing.
- Colour soft icing pink.
- Cover cake with soft icing.
- Position cake on board.
- Decorate cake as shown.

Press doily firmly and evenly onto unset surface of cake.

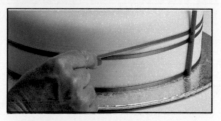

Secure bands of ribbon around cake with pins, join ends with sugar syrup. Remove pins when dry.

Secure lace around cake with pins, sew ends together; remove pins. Decorate cake with flowers.

graduation

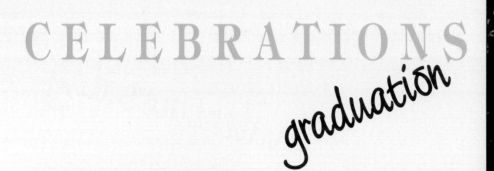

No.49

1 quantity fruit cake recipe
1 quantity almond icing
1 quantity soft icing
33cm round covered board
red, green, blue, brown and black colourings
braid
fibralo pens
sugar syrup
- Bake cake in deep 23cm round cake pan.
- Cover cake with almond icing.
- Cover cake with soft icing.
- Position cake on board.
- Decorate cake as shown.

Use scraps of soft icing to make books, mortar board, scroll, etc. Paint various colours when dry.

Secure braid around base of cake with pins, sew ends together; remove pins. Use pens to write messages on cake. Secure decorations onto cake with sugar syrup.

Graduation hat from The Trust Costume Shop

No.50

1 quantity fruit cake recipe
1 quantity almond icing
1 quantity soft icing
blue, green, yellow and orange colourings
30cm hexagonal covered board
sugar syrup
tracing wheel
green fibralo pen
polystyrene foam
braid
ribbon

- Bake cake in deep 20cm hexagonal cake pan.
- Cover cake with almond icing.
- Reserve a piece of soft icing about the size of a tennis ball.
- Colour remaining soft icing pale blue.
- Cover cake with blue soft icing.
- Position cake on board.
- Decorate cake as shown.

Colour scraps of soft icing for flowers, leaves and Star of David and cut out neatly. Use a little sugar syrup to position star on cake. Use tracing wheel to mark pattern on star. Arrange flowers and leaves on cake, use a little sugar syrup to hold them in position.

Use fibralo pen to mark in leaves and stems, etc.

Cut Star of David shape into a piece of polystyrene foam, use to press star impression around cake in unset icing.

Secure braid around cake with pins, sew ends together; remove pins. Secure ribbon around cake with pins, join ends with sugar syrup. Remove pins when dry.

Picture shows piece of polystyrene foam cut into Star of David shape.

Setting from The Avenue Gifts; card by courtesy of Hallmark Cards Aust Ltd

No.51

1 quantity fruit cake recipe
1 quantity almond icing
1 quantity soft icing
brown and blue colourings
27cm x 32cm rectangular covered board
sugar syrup
ribbon
greeting card
fibralo pen

- Bake cake in deep 17cm x 22cm rectangular cake pan.
- Cover cake with almond icing.
- Reserve a ball of soft icing about the size of a golf ball, colour blue; set aside.
- Colour soft icing off-white.
- Cover cake with off-white soft icing.
- Position cake on board.
- Decorate cake as shown.

Make a roll about 1cm in diameter from blue soft icing; secure around base of cake with a little sugar syrup. Mark pattern in unset soft icing with teaspoon.

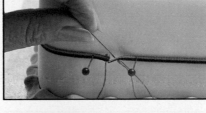

Secure ribbon around cake with pins, sew ends together; remove pins.

Brush the back of the cut-outs from card with a little sugar syrup, place in position on cake. Write greeting with fibralo pen.

Setting from The Avenue Gifts; card by courtesy of Hallmark Cards Aust Ltd

No.52

1 quantity fruit cake recipe
1 quantity almond icing
1 quantity soft icing
33cm octagonal covered board
yellow and green colourings
1 sheet gelatine
fibralo pens
ribbon
sugar syrup

- Bake cake in deep 23cm octagonal cake pan.
- Cover cake with almond icing.
- Cover cake with soft icing.
- Position cake on board.
- Decorate cake as shown.

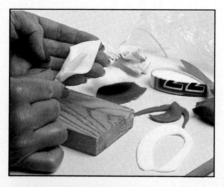

Colour a 2cm ball of soft icing scraps yellow; roll into cylinder shapes about 3cm long for the centres of the lilies. Leave to dry completely. For petals and leaves, make a cutter from a strip cut from an aluminium can, join ends with strong tape. These shapes can also be cut out with a sharp knife.

Roll out scraps of white soft icing, cut into petal shapes. Colour more scraps of soft icing green, cut out shapes for leaves. Twist into interesting shapes, leave to dry.

Cut out gelatine sheet to shape of window, use fibralo pens to mark in design and leaves. Place window in position on cake, decorate with lilies and leaves and a bow made from loops of ribbon. Sew loops together, cover joins with a centre made from green soft icing, attach with sugar syrup.

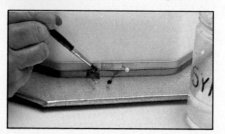

Secure ribbon around cake with pins, join ends with sugar syrup. Remove pins when dry.

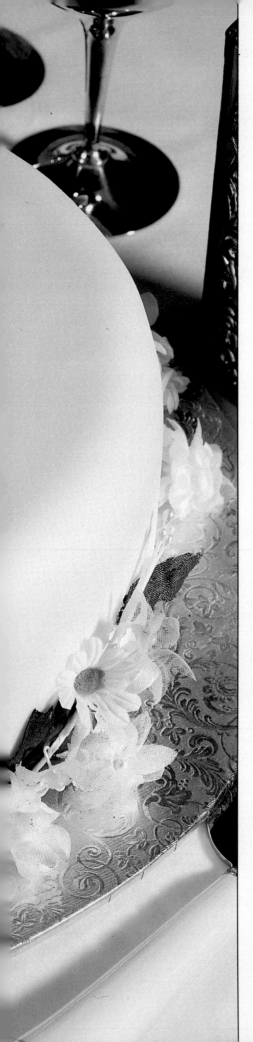

No.53

1 quantity fruit cake recipe
1 quantity almond icing
1 quantity soft icing
pink colouring
33cm round covered board
greeting card
sugar syrup
lace
artificial flowers

- Bake cake in deep 23cm round cake pan.
- Cover cake with almond icing.
- Colour soft icing pink.
- Cover cake with soft icing.
- Position cake on board
- Decorate cake as shown.

Brush back of cut-out from card lightly with sugar syrup, position on cake.

Measure lace around cut-out, secure to cake with sugar syrup. Hold in position with pins. Remove pins when dry.

Wire flowers together in sprays, arrange on cake as shown.

Cake server from Studio-Haus; Bible from Whitehill Silver

mother's day

No.54

1 quantity fruit cake recipe
1 quantity almond icing
1 quantity soft icing
pink colouring
28cm x 36cm oval covered board
lace
artificial flowers
patterned button
fibralo pen
ribbon

- Bake cake in deep 18cm x 26cm scalloped oval cake pan.
- Cover cake with almond icing.
- Reserve a ball of soft icing about 2cm in diameter.
- Colour remaining soft icing pink.
- Cover cake with pink soft icing.
- Position cake on board.
- Decorate cake as shown.

Loop gathered lace around cake, pin in each scallop. Use button to make pattern around cake in unset soft icing.

Remove pins, use stems of small flowers to hold lace in position.

Roll reserved soft icing into an oval shape, trim neatly. Smooth edge with fingers, position on cake. Write greeting with fibralo pen when soft icing is dry. Decorate top of cake with loops of ribbon and flowers.

Ice bucket from Whitehill Silver

CELEBRATIONS

mother's day

No.55

1 quantity fruit cake recipe
1 quantity almond icing
1 quantity soft icing
leaf green colouring
27cm x 32cm corner-cut rectangular covered board
lace with inserted ribbon
patterned button
sugar syrup
ribbon
artificial flowers

- Bake cake in deep 17cm x 22cm corner-cut rectangular cake pan.
- Cut corners off cake to give octagonal shape.
- Cover cake with almond icing.
- Colour soft icing green.
- Cover cake with soft icing.
- Position cake on board.
- Decorate cake as shown.

Push lace under cake as shown, stretch diagonally across cake, push end under other side of cake.

Picture shows button and shaped skewer used to decorate side of cake, do this before the icing is set.

Place ribbon around base of cake, secure with pins, join ends with sugar syrup; remove pins. Decorate top of cake with flowers and loops of ribbon.

Cloth from Balmain Linen & Lace

No.56

1½ quantities fruit cake recipe
apricot jam
1½ quantities almond icing
1½ quantities soft icing
brown, red, blue, black and yellow colourings
22cm x 68cm rectangular covered board
tracing wheel
sugar syrup

- Bake cake in deep 23cm square cake pan.
- Cut cake in half, join pieces end to end with sieved jam.
- Cover cake with almond icing.
- Reserve a piece of soft icing about the size of a tennis ball.
- Colour remaining soft icing brown.
- Cover joined cakes with brown soft icing.
- Position cake on board.
- Decorate cake as shown.

Make golf clubs and tees from reserved soft icing, leave shapes to dry flat on baking paper. Paint shapes when dry.

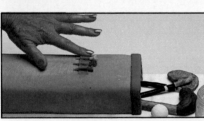

Position clubs as shown. Make a strap to hold tees from scraps of soft icing, secure strap in position with a little sugar syrup, put tees in position.

Make pouch and straps from soft icing scraps, as shown, position with a little sugar syrup, mark in "stitching" with a tracing wheel.

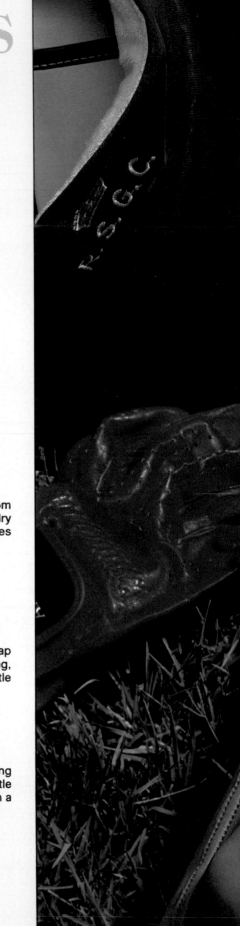

Out of Bounds

1. Ground outside Club boundary fences.

2. Area inside cottage grounds marked by pegs on which the words "out of bounds" are printed

Water Hazards

Creek in front of 3rd and 9t tees and behind 5th green

No.57

1 quantity fruit cake recipe
1 quantity almond icing
1 quantity soft icing
39cm round covered board
sugar syrup
cotton wool balls
tracing wheel
patterned button
thick black cotton
wool scraps
black marking pen

- Bake cake in deep 23cm round cake pan.
- Cover cake with almond icing.
- Position cake on board.
- Cover cake with soft icing, allowing enough icing to overhang on board to make brim of hat.
- Decorate cake as shown.

Make a band from soft icing scraps, secure around hat with sugar syrup. Use cotton wool balls to support curves in brim of hat. Use tracing wheel to mark unset soft icing to represent stitching. Use knife handle to press shape into crown of hat.

Mark "air holes" in crown of hat with button, paint when dry.

Cut thick black cotton into small pieces, dip in sugar syrup, twist cotton into hook shapes, or dry over a pencil.

Tie several pieces of wool together, comb until fluffy, as shown. Use black marking pen to pattern "flies".

CELEBRATIONS
debut

No.58

1½ quantities fruit cake recipe
1½ quantities almond icing
1½ quantities soft icing
blue colouring
35cm round covered board
fibralo pen
artificial flowers
ribbon
lace edging

- Bake cake in deep 25cm round cake pan.
- Cover cake with almond icing.
- Colour soft icing blue.
- Cover cake with soft icing.
- Position cake on board.
- Decorate cake as shown.

Write greeting in centre of cake. Make a tiny spray of flowers and ribbon loops for each debutante. Place half of them evenly on top of the cake and remaining half around side of cake. Push stems into unset soft icing to hold in position.

Using pins, position lace around cake, forming a zigzag from flower spray to flower spray, as shown. Sew lace edging to each spray; remove pins.

bon voyage

No.59

1 quantity fruit cake recipe
1 quantity almond icing
1 quantity soft icing
blue, green and yellow colourings
29cm square covered board
greeting card
sugar syrup

- Bake cake in deep 19cm square cake pan.
- Cover cake with almond icing.
- Colour soft icing pale blue.
- Cover cake with soft icing.
- Position cake on board.
- Decorate cake as shown.

Paint mountains on set surface of cake using green and yellow colourings. Use scraps of soft icing to make a roll large enough to wrap around cake. Place in position before colouring is dry. Use a fork to make pattern in soft icing, as shown; allow to dry.

Paint grass around cake, as shown.

Brush back of cut-out from card with a little sugar syrup, position on cake.

Lilliput Lane Handmade Cottages; quill from Studio-Haus; card by courtesy of Valentine Sands Greetings

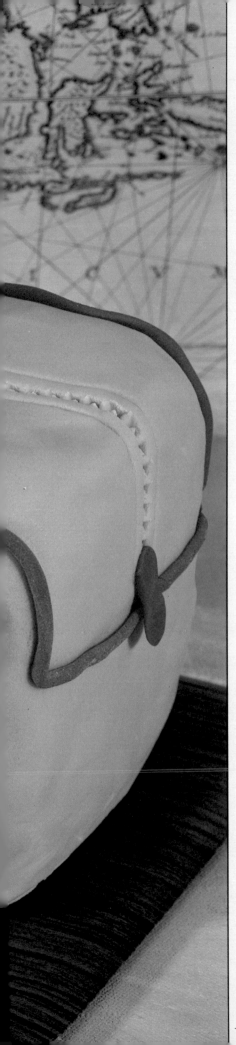

bon voyage

No.60

1½ quantities fruit cake recipe
apricot jam
1½ quantities almond icing
1½ quantities soft icing
orange and brown colourings
22cm x 33cm rectangular covered board
pastry wheel
sugar syrup
fibralo pens

- Bake cake in deep 23cm square cake pan.
- Cut cake in half vertically, join the 2 tops together with sieved jam to give shape of bag.
- Cover cake with almond icing.
- Reserve a piece of soft icing about the size of a tennis ball.
- Colour remaining soft icing tan with brown colouring.
- Cover cake with tan soft icing.
- Position cake on board.
- Decorate cake as shown.

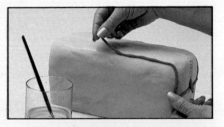

Use pastry wheel to mark in stitching on unset soft icing.

Colour a small piece of reserved soft icing orange, roll into thin sausage shapes. Secure to cake with sugar syrup to represent bindings, etc.

Colour about half the remaining reserved soft icing brown, cut strips long enough to tuck under bag and form handles; secure to cake with sugar syrup.

Picture shows pastry wheel used for marking in stitching. Cut out travel labels from remaining reserved soft icing, position on cake with a little sugar syrup. Write on labels with fibralo pens when dry.

bon voyage

No.61

Cake can be baked in a deep 30cm square cake pan, then cut out to the shape of Australia. You will need 2½ quantities fruit cake recipe if you use a 30cm square cake pan.

1½ quantities fruit cake recipe
1½ quantities almond icing
1½ quantities soft icing
37cm round covered board
brown colouring
ribbon
fibralo pen
fresh flowers

- Bake cake in deep 26cm x 27cm Australia cake pan.
- Cover cake with almond icing.
- Colour soft icing off-white.
- Cover cake with soft icing.
- Position cake on board.
- Decorate cake as shown.

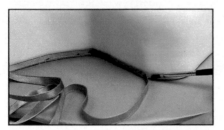

Secure ribbon around cake with pins, join ends with sugar syrup. Remove pins when dry.

Draw in the stars of the Southern Cross with fibralo pen. Decorate with flowers as late as possible.

Hat and riding accessories from The Trust Costume Shop

GLOSSARY

Here are some terms, names and alternatives to help everyone understand our methods.

Cornflour: cornstarch.

Glucose syrup (liquid glucose): is clear with a consistency like honey, it is made from wheat starch; available at health food stores and supermarkets. Do not confuse it with a glucose drink.

Icing sugar: also known as confectioners' sugar. It is used for making almond and soft icings. Dust your hands with it before handling the icings; also sprinkle some lightly on the surface you use for rolling out the icings as it absorbs stickiness. You must use pure icing sugar; buy it as close to using time as possible as it turns lumpy quickly. Sift finely just before using.

Jam: conserve.

Mixed peel: a mixture of chopped crystallised citrus peel.

Mixed spice: a finely ground combination of spices which include nutmeg, ginger and cinnamon; almost always used in sweet recipes. Do not confuse mixed spice with allspice (pimento) which is mostly used in savoury recipes.

Piping gel: is available from shops which specialise in cake decorators' supplies, it can be coloured as desired and piped or brushed where needed.

Plain flour: all-purpose flour.

Rice paper: is available from gourmet food shops and shops which specialise in Asian ingredients; it is edible.

Self-raising flour: substitute plain (all-purpose) flour and baking powder in the proportion of ¾ metric cup plain flour to 2 level metric teaspoons baking powder. Sift several times before using. If using an 8oz measuring cup, use 1 cup plain flour to 2 teaspoons baking powder.

Sheet gelatine: is available from some health food stores, delicatessens and gourmet food shops. Designs can be drawn on it with fibralo pens.

Sultanas: seedless white raisins.

RECIPES AND DECORATIONS

In this section are recipes for our famous rich fruit cake, for almond icing and soft icing, plus step-by-step tips to make decorating procedures simple and fun to do.

THE RICH FRUIT CAKE

We have used one of our favourite rich fruit cake recipes for all our decorated cakes; it gives a strong base to work on; however, you can use any fruit cake recipe of your choice.

CAKE COOKING TIMES

We have not specified cooking times for each cake as the times can vary depending on different factors, such as recipe, oven size, type and shape of cake pan used, and the type of fuel used for cooking.

As a guide, cook rich fruit cakes in a slow oven (150 degrees Celsius or 300 degrees Fahrenheit) for a minimum of 3 hours. Increase the time according to size and depth of mixture. Check the cake every 15 minutes.

TO TEST IF CAKE IS COOKED

Feel the surface of the cake; it should be firm to touch when it is cooked. Then, to make sure, use the blade of a sharp pointed knife (a long-bladed vegetable knife is ideal). Gently push the knife straight through the centre of the cake, right to the base of the pan.

Withdraw the knife slowly, then feel the blade with your fingers. If the blade shows uncooked mixture, return the cake to the oven for at least another 15 minutes. If it is free from mixture (don't confuse stickiness from fruit) it is cooked through.

TO COOL CAKE

Cover the top of the cake tightly with foil, turn the cake upside down on a board or bench; allow to come to room temperature. This can take up to 12 hours. Cooling the cake this way will help make the cake sit flat as sometimes the flat base of the cake is used for decorating.

TO STORE COOKED CAKE

When the cake is cold, remove from the pan. Discard brown paper, leave inner lining paper intact. Wrap cake tightly in plastic wrap to keep airtight, then in foil or tea-towels to keep the light out. Store in a cool dark place. If in doubt about hot or humid weather, store in refrigerator.

CELEBRATION FRUIT CAKE

Adapt quantity to suit individual cakes, as directed. this recipe is not suitable to microwave.

500g sultanas
250g raisins, chopped
125g dates, chopped
125g pitted prunes, chopped
125g currants
125g mixed peel
125g glacé cherries, chopped
60g glacé pineapple, chopped
60g glacé apricots, chopped
½ cup rum, brandy or sherry
250g butter
1 cup (250g) brown sugar,
    firmly packed
5 eggs
1¾ cups plain flour
⅓ cup self-raising flour
2 teaspoons mixed spice

Combine all fruit in large bowl with rum; mix well, cover to keep airtight; stand for a week, stir occasionally.

Beat butter in small bowl with electric mixer until just soft, add sugar, beat only until combined. Add eggs quickly, 1 at a time, beating only until mixture is combined between each addition. Stir creamed mixture into fruit mixture. Stir in sifted dry ingredients in 2 batches. Spread evenly into prepared pan, bake as directed.

This quantity of fruit cake will cut into about 50 pieces. A double mixture will cut into about 100 pieces.

CAKE PANS

CAKE PAN SIZES

We have specified the sizes of cake pans and the quantities required to make your cakes look the same as ours; however, cake sizes and shapes can be changed to suit yourself and your chosen decorations.

Use well-shaped, rigid, straight-sided deep cake pans. The ones we used are made from good quality tin or aluminium.

We used cake pans bought from shops specialising in cake decorating equipment.

TO LINE CAKE PANS

There are many different ideas about lining cake pans; all work well if done neatly and properly. This step will minimise wasteful and time-consuming trimming and patching of cakes.

We used 2 layers of thick brown paper with a layer of baking paper inside. Always bring the paper at least 2cm above the edge of the pan; this helps to protect the top of the cake during the cooking. Cut paper at base of pan at an angle as shown so that paper fits cake pan corners neatly.

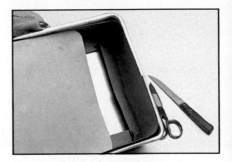

UNUSUAL SHAPED CAKES

Unusual-shaped cakes such as heart, oval, scallop, octagonal, hexagonal and petal-shaped, etc. can all be cut from round cakes.

From a square cake you can easily cut diamond, rectangular, corner-cut rectangular and Australia.

A book-shaped cake can be made by making 2 quantities fruit cake recipe and baking them in 2 deep rectangular cake pans measuring 22cm x 27cm.

Cut the cakes to shape.

Use a template made from brown paper for the pattern. Use a sharp knife for best results, cut as shown.

Picture shows a variety of templates folded and cut to desired shape, then used for cutting out cakes.

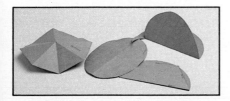

A key-shaped cake can be made by making 1½ quantities fruit cake recipe and dividing it between a deep 20cm round cake pan and a deep 15cm square cake pan. Cut the square cake as shown in picture. Join the trimmed round cake to the pieces of square cake with sieved apricot jam.

COVERING CAKES

Cakes are covered first with almond icing then soft icing before they are decorated. Almond icing and soft icing must be kept covered while not being handled as the air makes a crust develop. Keep wrapped tightly in plastic or store in an airtight container.

Both these icings will keep for at least a week in the refrigerator.

ALMOND ICING

We prefer to grind our own almonds finely for this recipe; do this in a blender or processor.

Ideally, almond-icing-covered cakes need to stand for 1 day at room temperature before they are covered with soft icing.

If using packaged commercial almond icing, you will need to use 750g

to make it equivalent to 1 quantity of this almond icing recipe.

500g (2 cups) pure icing sugar, sifted
125g blanched almond kernels, ground
2 tablespoons brandy
2 egg yolks
1 teaspoon lemon juice

Mix icing sugar and almonds together in large bowl, make well in centre, stir in combined brandy, egg yolks and lemon juice.

HOW TO COVER CAKE WITH ALMOND ICING

Mix a little soft icing and boiled water to a sticky paste. Spread about a heaped tablespoon of this mixture onto a sheet of greaseproof paper larger than the cake. Position cake on top. Use a spatula or flexible knife blade and small pieces of almond icing to patch any holes in the cake's surface, top and sides.

Knead the almond icing gently until smooth, using a little sifted icing sugar to absorb stickiness. Roll it out to about 7mm thick. Measure the sides of the cake, cut 3 or 4 strips large enough to fit the sides. When covering a square cake, wrap the strips around the corners. Attach the icing to cake after brushing surface of almond icing evenly all over with sugar syrup.

Use the base of the cake pan as a pattern to measure a piece of almond icing for the top of the cake.

Lift the top piece into place, and rub over the joins to seal them together. Leave cake standing on the greaseproof paper.

SOFT ICING

If using packaged commercial soft-icing, you will need to use 750g to make it equivalent to 1 quantity of this soft icing recipe

Soft-icing-covered cakes need to be left to dry for at least 2 days, depending on the weather. Some of the cakes in this book need to be decorated with the icing unset; others require it to be firm or completely set. Follow individual recipes.

2 tablespoons water
3 teaspoons gelatine
2 tablespoons glucose syrup
2 teaspoons glycerine
500g (2 cups) pure icing sugar, sifted
about ¾ cup pure icing sugar, sifted, extra

Place water in small saucepan, add gelatine, stir over low heat until gelatine is dissolved; do not boil. Remove from heat, stir in glucose syrup and glycerine, cool to warm.

Place icing sugar into large bowl, make well in centre, gradually stir in liquid. When mixture becomes too stiff to stir, mix with hand. Turn icing onto surface which has been well dusted with some of the extra sifted icing sugar. Knead lightly and gently until smooth, pliable and without stickiness.

HOW TO COVER CAKE WITH SOFT ICING

Brush almond icing lightly but evenly with sugar syrup. Knead soft icing with more extra sifted icing sugar until smooth, roll out evenly to about 7mm thick. Lift onto cake with rolling pin or piece of plastic pipe, as shown in picture below.

Smooth the icing with hands dusted with extra icing sugar, ease the icing around the sides and base of cake.

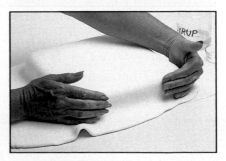

Push icing in around the base, cut away excess icing with a sharp knife.

Mix some scraps of soft icing to a sticky paste with cold boiled water. You need about 2 level tablespoons of this paste.

Spread paste in the centre of the prepared board. Place cake on board.

Move the cake to the correct position on the board, cut away the greaseproof paper carefully around the cake using a sharp knife or scalpel.

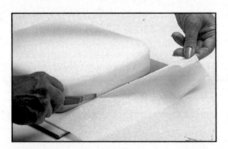

SUGAR SYRUP

This quantity of syrup will make enough for you to use when applying almond and soft icings to the cake, and leave enough to use for attaching decorations, etc.

Combine ½ cup water, ½ cup white sugar and 1 teaspoon glucose syrup in a small saucepan. Stir constantly over high heat, without boiling, until sugar is dissolved. Bring to the boil, reduce heat, simmer, without stirring, for 5 minutes; cool to room temperature. Store, covered, in a jar at room temperature for up to 2 weeks.

HOW TO STORE DECORATED CAKES

Cakes need to be protected from moisture in the air, either rain or humidity or, worse, both. If possible, keep the cake in a cabinet or under glass or plastic so you can check for changes in the cake's appearance.

If the surface becomes wet and sticky, remove the cake from the cabinet and stand it under an ordinary reading lamp (not fluorescent). Turn the cake every now and then until the icing looks and feels dry, then return it to the cabinet.

Decorated cakes can be frozen if they are to be kept for more than 3 months. Thaw the cake, covered, in the refrigerator. This will take about 2 days.

HOW TO TRANSPORT CAKES

Cakes can be transported easily by placing them on a piece of thin sponge rubber (to prevent slipping) in a box as close to the size of the board as possible. Cover an open box with clear plastic, sit box flat.

Tiered cakes are always transported with the tiers separated, and assembled when they reach their destination.

COLOURINGS

We have used liquid food colourings throughout this book. Buy good brands as they will give you better colours and you won't have to use as much as the cheaper brands. Always use a tiny amount at a time until you gauge the strength and intensity of colour required.

When using these colourings for painting, they can be used straight from the bottle or diluted with water.

Reserve scraps of soft icing, leave to dry, then use for testing colours before painting the real thing.

Edible paste colour concentrate is an imported product available from shops specialising in cake decorating supplies and large department stores. These are easy to handle and are mostly used when a more intense colour is required for soft icing.

COVERING CAKE BOARDS

It is important to cover cake boards neatly. There are many different materials available to use, such as paper, fabric and Contact plastic.

We used Masonite about 5mm thick for our boards.

Spread several sheets of newspaper on a bench, cut covering material 3cm larger all round than the board. Place covering material on newspaper, position board as shown. Spray board with glue.

Picture shows how to cover square board correctly.

Picture shows how to cut covering paper to fit neatly around the curve of a round board.

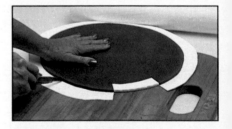

Picture shows how to make supports for boards from Masonite scraps.

Picture shows how to cover a board with fabric. Sew a gathering stitch around a circle of fabric, place over board (cover the board with Contact plastic first if the fabric is thin), gather edge and tie tightly.

DECORATIONS

These simple tips will help you to secure ribbons and lace, trace designs onto your cakes, write messages and decorate cakes with flowers and candles, as preferred.

Individual recipes in the book also include fabulous novelty patterns to make using buttons, spoon handles, the prongs of a fork, and more.

SECURING RIBBONS, BRAID AND LACE, ETC.

It is often easier to secure ribbon, braid and lace, etc. around the cake before the icing is set; it can be pulled quite tight and the ends joined neatly. As a general rule, ribbon ends can be held with pins and joined with syrup, then the pins removed when the ends are dry. Egg white can be used instead of sugar syrup, if preferred.

Braid and lace ends are generally too heavy for the syrup to hold and need to be sewn together; a curved needle is handy for this. We used pins with large coloured heads for easy visibility and removal. Dressmakers' pins are easy to lose and must be avoided to prevent accidents.

POSITIONING RIBBONS, BRAID AND LACE, ETC.

Use something like a cotton reel as a guide to mark where ribbons, braid or lace, etc. are to be positioned.

TRACING

Tracing is an easy and effective decoration, using cards and pictures as a guide.

Place greaseproof paper over the picture and trace outline with a pencil.

Place tracing, pencilled-side-down, on surface of set soft icing, draw over tracing with pencil, as shown, to produce picture on cake's surface.

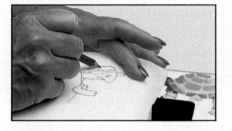

Colour in tracing with fibralo pens or paint with food colourings or piping gel depending on desired effect.

FIBRALO PENS

These are a great help to draw patterns, colour in areas and write messages, etc. on cakes and decorations. There are several brands of these non-toxic pens available.

Picture shows a design being traced from a card using different coloured pens.

SILK FLOWERS

Silk flowers can be used in several ways. They can be pulled from their stems and gently pushed into unset icing. Or they can be placed on a double piece of wire, as shown.

Then they can be wired with other flowers and taped together with florist's plastic tape to make sprays or posies, etc.

FRESH FLOWERS

Fresh flowers always look wonderful and can be arranged at home at the last minute, or you can have them arranged by a florist. In this case, collect them as late as possible and make sure you explain clearly to the florist how the flowers are to be arranged on the cake.

Keep any arrangements in the refrigerator. Make sure flowers are dry before they are placed on cake because drops of water will mark the soft icing.

Avoid pushing wired flowers into the cake, as it is extremely easy to cut through wire and cut it into small dangerous particles.

All fresh flowers in this book were arranged by Helen Tremain, of Frenchs Forest, Sydney.

CANDLES

The easiest way to fix candles to a cake is to push them into the unset soft icing. Alternatively, buy plastic candle holders and push the holders into the soft icing (set or unset).

QUICK CONVERSION GUIDE

Wherever you live in the world, you can use our recipes with the help of our easy-to-follow conversions for all your cooking needs. These conversions are approximate only. The difference between the exact and approximate conversions of liquid and dry measures amounts to only a teaspoon or two, and will not make any noticeable difference to your cooking results.

MEASURING EQUIPMENT

The difference between measuring cups internationally is minimal within 2 or 3 teaspoons' difference. (For the record, 1 Australian metric measuring cup will hold approximately 250ml.) The most accurate way of measuring dry ingredients is to weigh them. When measuring liquids use a clear glass or plastic jug with metric markings.

In this book we use metric measuring cups and spoons approved by Standards Australia.

● a graduated set of 4 cups for measuring dry ingredients; the sizes are marked on the cups.
● a graduated set of 4 spoons for measuring dry and liquid ingredients; the amounts are marked on the spoons.
● 1 TEASPOON: 5ml
● 1 TABLESPOON: 20ml

**NOTE: NZ, CANADA, USA AND UK ALL USE 15ml TABLESPOONS.
ALL CUP AND SPOON MEASUREMENTS ARE LEVEL.**

DRY MEASURES

METRIC	IMPERIAL
15g	½oz
30g	1oz
60g	2oz
90g	3oz
125g	4oz (¼lb)
155g	5oz
185g	6oz
220g	7oz
250g	8oz (½lb)
280g	9oz
315g	10oz
345g	11oz
375g	12oz (¾lb)
410g	13oz
440g	14oz
470g	15oz
500g	16oz (1lb)
750g	24oz (1½lb)
1kg	32oz (2lb)

LIQUID MEASURES

METRIC	IMPERIAL
30ml	1 fluid oz
60ml	2 fluid oz
100ml	3 fluid oz
125ml	4 fluid oz
150ml	5 fluid oz (¼ pint/1 gill)
190ml	6 fluid oz
250ml	8 fluid oz
300ml	10 fluid oz (½ pint)
500ml	16 fluid oz
600ml	20 fluid oz (1 pint)
1000ml (1 litre)	1¾ pints

**WE USE LARGE EGGS
WITH AN AVERAGE
WEIGHT OF 60g**

HELPFUL MEASURES

METRIC	IMPERIAL
3mm	⅛in
6mm	¼in
1cm	½in
2cm	¾in
2.5cm	1in
5cm	2in
6cm	2½in
8cm	3in
10cm	4in
13cm	5in
15cm	6in
18cm	7in
20cm	8in
23cm	9in
25cm	10in
28cm	11in
30cm	12in (1ft)

HOW TO MEASURE

When using the graduated metric measuring cups, it is important to shake the dry ingredients loosely into the required cup. Do not tap the cup on the bench, or pack the ingredients into the cup unless otherwise directed. Level top of cup with knife. When using graduated metric measuring spoons, level top of spoon with knife. When measuring liquids in the jug, place jug on flat surface, check for accuracy at eye level.

OVEN TEMPERATURES

These oven temperatures are only a guide; we've given you the lower degree of heat. Always check the manufacturer's manual.

	C˙ (Celsius)	F˙ (Fahrenheit)	Gas Mark
Very slow	120	250	1
Slow	150	300	2
Moderately slow	160	325	3
Moderate	180	350	4
Moderately hot	190	375	5
Hot	200	400	6
Very hot	230	450	7